Caravan Logbook

Caravan Name:

_____

_____

_____

Copyright © 2019 by Vita Rae Publishing

All rights reserved. This book or any portion thereof
may not be reproduced or used in any manner whatsoever
without the express written permission of the publisher
except for the use of brief quotations in a book review.

First Printing, 2019

Contact: vitaraepublishing@yahoo.com

Website: www.vitaraepublishing.com

Campground Name _____

Address _____

Website _____ Email _____

Phone _____ Hours _____

Category

☐ National Park   ☐ County Park   ☐ Private   ☐ Army Corp. of Eng.

☐ State Park   ☐ BLM   ☐ Province/Parish   ☐ Other _____

Rates ($, £ , €) (circle one)

Daily _____   Monthly _____

Weekly _____   Long Stay _____

Services   Toilets   Showers

☐ Electric   Amp _____   ☐ Pit   ☐ None   ☐ Yes

☐ Water   ☐ Dump Station   ☐ Composting   ☐ No

☐ Sewer   ☐ Water Pressure ☺ ☹   ☐ Flush

Security

☐ Attendant - Hours _____   ☐ Gates

☐ Camp Host - Hours _____   Lock Out Times _____

                                           Opening _____ Closing _____

Connectivity   Signal Quality (circle one)

☐ WiFi   ☐ Free   ☐ Fee _____

☐ Cell Service   Carrier _____

☐ TV   ☐ Free   ☐ Fee _____

Facilities

☐ Laundry   Cost _____   ☐ Gym   ☐ Free   ☐ Fee _____

☐ Pool   ☐ Hot Tub   ☐ Club House   ☐ Free   ☐ Fee _____

☐ Boating   ☐ Pet Friendly - ☐ Free   ☐ Fee _____

Food Options   Kids Activities

☐ Groceries   ☐ Restaurants   ☐ Playground   ☐ Parks

☐ Snack Bar   ☐ Other Shops

Local Highlights

Things to do/Recommendations

Rating (choose 1 to 5 🔥)

Notes

Campground Name _____

Address _____

Website _____ Email _____

Phone _____ Hours _____

Category

- ☐ National Park
- ☐ County Park
- ☐ Private
- ☐ Army Corp. of Eng.
- ☐ State Park
- ☐ BLM
- ☐ Province/Parish
- ☐ Other _____

Rates ($, £ , €) (circle one)

Daily _____ Monthly _____

Weekly _____ Long Stay _____

Services

- ☐ Electric   Amp_____
- ☐ Water   ☐ Dump Station
- ☐ Sewer   ☐ Water Pressure ☺ ☹

Toilets
- ☐ Pit
- ☐ Composting
- ☐ Flush

Showers
- ☐ None   ☐ Yes
- ☐ No

Security

- ☐ Attendant - Hours _____
- ☐ Camp Host - Hours _____
- ☐ Gates
- Lock Out Times _____
- Opening _____ Closing _____

Connectivity

- ☐ WiFi   ☐ Free   ☐ Fee _____
- ☐ Cell Service   Carrier _____
- ☐ TV   ☐ Free   ☐ Fee _____

Signal Quality (circle one)

Facilities

- ☐ Laundry   Cost _____
- ☐ Pool   ☐ Hot Tub
- ☐ Boating   ☐ Pet Friendly - ☐ Free   ☐ Fee _____
- ☐ Gym   ☐ Free   ☐ Fee _____
- ☐ Club House ☐ Free   ☐ Fee _____

Food Options

- ☐ Groceries   ☐ Restaurants
- ☐ Snack Bar   ☐ Other Shops

Kids Activities

- ☐ Playground   ☐ Parks

Local Highlights

Things to do/Recommendations

Rating (choose 1 to 5 🔥)

🔥 🔥 🔥 🔥 🔥 🔥

Notes

Campground Name _____

Address _____

Website _____ Email _____

Phone _____ Hours _____

Category

- [ ] National Park
- [ ] County Park
- [ ] Private
- [ ] Army Corp. of Eng.
- [ ] State Park
- [ ] BLM
- [ ] Province/Parish
- [ ] Other _____

Rates ($, £ , €) (circle one)

Daily _____ Monthly _____

Weekly _____ Long Stay _____

Services   Toilets   Showers

- [ ] Electric   Amp_____
- [ ] Pit   [ ] None   [ ] Yes
- [ ] Water   [ ] Dump Station
- [ ] Composting   [ ] No
- [ ] Sewer   [ ] Water Pressure ☺ ☹
- [ ] Flush

Security

- [ ] Attendant - Hours _____   [ ] Gates
- [ ] Camp Host - Hours _____

Lock Out Times _____

Opening _____   Closing _____

Connectivity   Signal Quality (circle one)

- [ ] WiFi   [ ] Free   [ ] Fee _____
- [ ] Cell Service   Carrier _____
- [ ] TV   [ ] Free   [ ] Fee _____

Facilities

- [ ] Laundry   Cost _____
- [ ] Gym   [ ] Free   [ ] Fee _____
- [ ] Pool   [ ] Hot Tub
- [ ] Club House   [ ] Free   [ ] Fee _____
- [ ] Boating   [ ] Pet Friendly -   [ ] Free   [ ] Fee _____

Food Options   Kids Activities

- [ ] Groceries   [ ] Restaurants
- [ ] Playground   [ ] Parks
- [ ] Snack Bar   [ ] Other Shops

Local Highlights

Things to do/Recommendations

Rating (choose 1 to 5 🔥)

Notes

Campground Name _____

Address _____

Website _____ Email _____

Phone _____ Hours _____

Category

☐ National Park ☐ County Park ☐ Private ☐ Army Corp. of Eng.

☐ State Park ☐ BLM ☐ Province/Parish ☐ Other _____

Rates ($, £ , €) (circle one)

Daily _____ Monthly _____

Weekly _____ Long Stay _____

Services

		Toilets		Showers
☐ Electric	Amp _____	☐ Pit	☐ None	☐ Yes
☐ Water	☐ Dump Station	☐ Composting		☐ No
☐ Sewer	☐ Water Pressure ☺ ☹	☐ Flush		

Security

☐ Attendant - Hours _____ ☐ Gates

☐ Camp Host - Hours _____ Lock Out Times _____

Opening _____ Closing _____

Connectivity

Signal Quality (circle one)

☐ WiFi ☐ Free ☐ Fee _____

☐ Cell Service Carrier _____

☐ TV ☐ Free ☐ Fee _____

Facilities

☐ Laundry Cost _____

☐ Pool ☐ Hot Tub

☐ Boating ☐ Pet Friendly - ☐ Free ☐ Fee _____

☐ Gym ☐ Free ☐ Fee _____

☐ Club House ☐ Free ☐ Fee _____

Food Options

☐ Groceries ☐ Restaurants

☐ Snack Bar ☐ Other Shops

Kids Activities

☐ Playground ☐ Parks

Local Highlights

Things to do/Recommendations

Rating (choose 1 to 5 🔥)

Notes

Campground Name _____

Address _____

Website _____ Email _____

Phone _____ Hours _____

Category

- ☐ National Park
- ☐ County Park
- ☐ Private
- ☐ Army Corp. of Eng.
- ☐ State Park
- ☐ BLM
- ☐ Province/Parish
- ☐ Other _____

Rates ($, £ , €) (circle one)

Daily _____ Monthly _____

Weekly _____ Long Stay _____

Services   Toilets   Showers

- ☐ Electric   Amp_____   ☐ Pit   ☐ None   ☐ Yes
- ☐ Water   ☐ Dump Station   ☐ Composting   ☐ No
- ☐ Sewer   ☐ Water Pressure ☺ ☹   ☐ Flush

Security

- ☐ Attendant - Hours _____   ☐ Gates
- ☐ Camp Host - Hours _____   Lock Out Times _____
- Opening _____ Closing _____

Connectivity   Signal Quality (circle one)

- ☐ WiFi   ☐ Free   ☐ Fee _____
- ☐ Cell Service   Carrier _____
- ☐ TV   ☐ Free   ☐ Fee _____

Facilities

- ☐ Laundry   Cost _____   ☐ Gym   ☐ Free   ☐ Fee _____
- ☐ Pool   ☐ Hot Tub   ☐ Club House   ☐ Free   ☐ Fee _____
- ☐ Boating   ☐ Pet Friendly -   ☐ Free   ☐ Fee _____

Food Options   Kids Activities

- ☐ Groceries   ☐ Restaurants   ☐ Playground   ☐ Parks
- ☐ Snack Bar   ☐ Other Shops

Local Highlights

Things to do/Recommendations

Rating (choose 1 to 5 🔥)

🔥 🔥 🔥 🔥 🔥

Notes

Campground Name _____

Address _____

Website _____ Email _____

Phone _____ Hours _____

Category

- ☐ National Park
- ☐ County Park
- ☐ Private
- ☐ Army Corp. of Eng.
- ☐ State Park
- ☐ BLM
- ☐ Province/Parish
- ☐ Other _____

Rates ($, £ , €) (circle one)

Daily _____ Monthly _____

Weekly _____ Long Stay _____

Services

		Toilets		Showers
☐ Electric	Amp_____	☐ Pit	☐ None	☐ Yes
☐ Water	☐ Dump Station	☐ Composting		☐ No
☐ Sewer	☐ Water Pressure ☺ ☹	☐ Flush		

Security

- ☐ Attendant - Hours _____
- ☐ Gates
- ☐ Camp Host - Hours _____
- Lock Out Times _____
- Opening _____ Closing _____

Connectivity

Signal Quality (circle one)

- ☐ WiFi   ☐ Free   ☐ Fee _____
- ☐ Cell Service   Carrier _____
- ☐ TV   ☐ Free   ☐ Fee _____

Facilities

- ☐ Laundry   Cost _____
- ☐ Gym   ☐ Free   ☐ Fee _____
- ☐ Pool   ☐ Hot Tub
- ☐ Club House   ☐ Free   ☐ Fee _____
- ☐ Boating   ☐ Pet Friendly -   ☐ Free   ☐ Fee _____

Food Options

- ☐ Groceries   ☐ Restaurants
- ☐ Snack Bar   ☐ Other Shops

Kids Activities

- ☐ Playground   ☐ Parks

Local Highlights

Things to do/Recommendations

Rating (choose 1 to 5 🔥)

Notes

Campground Name _____

Address _____

Website _____ Email _____

Phone _____ Hours _____

Category

☐ National Park   ☐ County Park   ☐ Private   ☐ Army Corp. of Eng.

☐ State Park   ☐ BLM   ☐ Province/Parish   ☐ Other _____

Rates ($, £ , €) (circle one)

Daily _____ Monthly _____

Weekly _____ Long Stay _____

Services   Toilets   Showers

☐ Electric   Amp _____   ☐ Pit   ☐ None   ☐ Yes

☐ Water   ☐ Dump Station   ☐ Composting   ☐ No

☐ Sewer   ☐ Water Pressure ☺ ☹   ☐ Flush

Security

☐ Attendant - Hours _____   ☐ Gates

☐ Camp Host - Hours _____   Lock Out Times _____

Opening _____   Closing _____

Connectivity   Signal Quality (circle one)

☐ WiFi   ☐ Free   ☐ Fee _____

☐ Cell Service   Carrier _____

☐ TV   ☐ Free   ☐ Fee _____

Facilities

☐ Laundry   Cost _____   ☐ Gym   ☐ Free   ☐ Fee _____

☐ Pool   ☐ Hot Tub   ☐ Club House   ☐ Free   ☐ Fee _____

☐ Boating   ☐ Pet Friendly -   ☐ Free   ☐ Fee _____

Food Options   Kids Activities

☐ Groceries   ☐ Restaurants   ☐ Playground   ☐ Parks

☐ Snack Bar   ☐ Other Shops

Local Highlights

Things to do/Recommendations

Rating (choose 1 to 5 🔥)

🔥 🔥 🔥 🔥 🔥 🔥

Notes

Campground Name _____

Address _____

Website _____ Email _____

Phone _____ Hours _____

Category

☐ National Park   ☐ County Park   ☐ Private   ☐ Army Corp. of Eng.

☐ State Park   ☐ BLM   ☐ Province/Parish   ☐ Other _____

Rates ($, £ , €) (circle one)

Daily _____   Monthly _____

Weekly _____   Long Stay _____

Services   Toilets   Showers

☐ Electric   Amp _____   ☐ Pit   ☐ None   ☐ Yes

☐ Water   ☐ Dump Station   ☐ Composting   ☐ No

☐ Sewer   ☐ Water Pressure ☺ ☹   ☐ Flush

Security

☐ Attendant - Hours _____   ☐ Gates

☐ Camp Host - Hours _____   Lock Out Times _____

                                          Opening _____   Closing _____

Connectivity   Signal Quality (circle one)

☐ WiFi   ☐ Free   ☐ Fee _____

☐ Cell Service Carrier _____

☐ TV   ☐ Free   ☐ Fee _____

Facilities

☐ Laundry   Cost _____   ☐ Gym   ☐ Free   ☐ Fee _____

☐ Pool   ☐ Hot Tub   ☐ Club House   ☐ Free   ☐ Fee _____

☐ Boating   ☐ Pet Friendly - ☐ Free ☐ Fee _____

Food Options   Kids Activities

☐ Groceries   ☐ Restaurants   ☐ Playground   ☐ Parks

☐ Snack Bar   ☐ Other Shops

Local Highlights

Things to do/Recommendations

Rating (choose 1 to 5 🔥)

🔥 🔥 🔥 🔥 🔥

Notes

Campground Name _____

Address _____

Website _____ Email _____

Phone _____ Hours _____

Category

- ☐ National Park
- ☐ County Park
- ☐ Private
- ☐ Army Corp. of Eng.
- ☐ State Park
- ☐ BLM
- ☐ Province/Parish
- ☐ Other _____

Rates ($, £ , €) (circle one)

Daily _____ Monthly _____

Weekly _____ Long Stay _____

Services   Toilets   Showers

- ☐ Electric   Amp_____   ☐ Pit   ☐ None   ☐ Yes
- ☐ Water   ☐ Dump Station ☐ Composting   ☐ No
- ☐ Sewer   ☐ Water Pressure ☺ ☹   ☐ Flush

Security

- ☐ Attendant - Hours _____   ☐ Gates
- ☐ Camp Host - Hours _____   Lock Out Times _____

  Opening _____ Closing _____

Connectivity   Signal Quality (circle one)

- ☐ WiFi   ☐ Free   ☐ Fee _____
- ☐ Cell Service Carrier _____
- ☐ TV   ☐ Free   ☐ Fee _____

Facilities

- ☐ Laundry   Cost _____   ☐ Gym   ☐ Free   ☐ Fee _____
- ☐ Pool   ☐ Hot Tub   ☐ Club House   ☐ Free   ☐ Fee _____
- ☐ Boating   ☐ Pet Friendly - ☐ Free   ☐ Fee _____

Food Options   Kids Activities

- ☐ Groceries   ☐ Restaurants   ☐ Playground   ☐ Parks
- ☐ Snack Bar   ☐ Other Shops

Local Highlights

Things to do/Recommendations

Rating (choose 1 to 5 🔥)

🔥 🔥 🔥 🔥 🔥

Notes

Campground Name _____

Address _____

Website _____ Email _____

Phone _____ Hours _____

Category

☐ National Park ☐ County Park ☐ Private ☐ Army Corp. of Eng.

☐ State Park ☐ BLM ☐ Province/Parish ☐ Other _____

Rates ($, £ , €) (circle one)

Daily _____ Monthly _____

Weekly _____ Long Stay _____

Services Toilets Showers

☐ Electric Amp_____ ☐ Pit ☐ None ☐ Yes

☐ Water ☐ Dump Station ☐ Composting ☐ No

☐ Sewer ☐ Water Pressure 🙂 ☹ ☐ Flush

Security

☐ Attendant - Hours _____ ☐ Gates

☐ Camp Host - Hours _____ Lock Out Times _____

Opening _____ Closing _____

Connectivity Signal Quality (circle one)

☐ WiFi ☐ Free ☐ Fee _____

☐ Cell Service Carrier _____

☐ TV ☐ Free ☐ Fee _____

Facilities

☐ Laundry Cost _____ ☐ Gym ☐ Free ☐ Fee _____

☐ Pool ☐ Hot Tub ☐ Club House ☐ Free ☐ Fee _____

☐ Boating ☐ Pet Friendly - ☐ Free ☐ Fee _____

Food Options Kids Activities

☐ Groceries ☐ Restaurants ☐ Playground ☐ Parks

☐ Snack Bar ☐ Other Shops

Local Highlights

Things to do/Recommendations

Rating (choose 1 to 5 🔥)

🔥 🔥 🔥 🔥 🔥 🔥

Notes

Campground Name _____
Address _____

| Website _____ | Email _____ |
| Phone _____ | Hours _____ |

Category

- ☐ National Park
- ☐ County Park
- ☐ Private
- ☐ Army Corp. of Eng.
- ☐ State Park
- ☐ BLM
- ☐ Province/Parish
- ☐ Other _____

Rates ($, £ , €) (circle one)

| Daily _____ | Monthly _____ |
| Weekly _____ | Long Stay _____ |

Services   Toilets   Showers

- ☐ Electric   Amp_____   ☐ Pit   ☐ None   ☐ Yes
- ☐ Water   ☐ Dump Station   ☐ Composting   ☐ No
- ☐ Sewer   ☐ Water Pressure 🙂 🙁   ☐ Flush

Security

- ☐ Attendant - Hours_____   ☐ Gates
- ☐ Camp Host - Hours_____   Lock Out Times _____
  Opening_____   Closing_____

Connectivity   Signal Quality (circle one)

- ☐ WiFi   ☐ Free   ☐ Fee _____
- ☐ Cell Service   Carrier _____
- ☐ TV   ☐ Free   ☐ Fee _____

Facilities

- ☐ Laundry   Cost _____   ☐ Gym   ☐ Free   ☐ Fee _____
- ☐ Pool   ☐ Hot Tub   ☐ Club House   ☐ Free   ☐ Fee _____
- ☐ Boating   ☐ Pet Friendly - ☐ Free ☐ Fee _____

Food Options   Kids Activities

- ☐ Groceries   ☐ Restaurants   ☐ Playground   ☐ Parks
- ☐ Snack Bar   ☐ Other Shops

Local Highlights

Things to do/Recommendations

Rating (choose 1 to 5 🔥)

🔥 🔥 🔥 🔥 🔥 🔥

Notes

Campground Name _____

Address _____

Website _____ Email _____

Phone _____ Hours _____

Category

☐ National Park   ☐ County Park   ☐ Private   ☐ Army Corp. of Eng.

☐ State Park   ☐ BLM   ☐ Province/Parish   ☐ Other _____

Rates ($, £ , €) (circle one)

Daily _____   Monthly _____

Weekly _____   Long Stay _____

Services   Toilets   Showers

☐ Electric   Amp_____   ☐ Pit   ☐ None   ☐ Yes

☐ Water   ☐ Dump Station   ☐ Composting   ☐ No

☐ Sewer   ☐ Water Pressure ☺ ☹   ☐ Flush

Security

☐ Attendant - Hours _____   ☐ Gates

☐ Camp Host - Hours _____   Lock Out Times _____

                                         Opening _____   Closing _____

Connectivity   Signal Quality (circle one)

☐ WiFi   ☐ Free   ☐ Fee _____

☐ Cell Service   Carrier _____

☐ TV   ☐ Free   ☐ Fee _____

Facilities

☐ Laundry   Cost _____   ☐ Gym   ☐ Free   ☐ Fee _____

☐ Pool   ☐ Hot Tub   ☐ Club House   ☐ Free   ☐ Fee _____

☐ Boating   ☐ Pet Friendly - ☐ Free   ☐ Fee _____

Food Options   Kids Activities

☐ Groceries   ☐ Restaurants   ☐ Playground   ☐ Parks

☐ Snack Bar   ☐ Other Shops

Local Highlights

Things to do/Recommendations

Rating (choose 1 to 5 🔥)

🔥 🔥 🔥 🔥 🔥

Notes

Campground Name _____

Address _____

Website _____ Email _____

Phone _____ Hours _____

Category

☐ National Park ☐ County Park ☐ Private ☐ Army Corp. of Eng.

☐ State Park ☐ BLM ☐ Province/Parish ☐ Other _____

Rates ($, £ , €) (circle one)

Daily _____ Monthly _____

Weekly _____ Long Stay _____

Services   Toilets   Showers

☐ Electric   Amp_____   ☐ Pit   ☐ None   ☐ Yes

☐ Water   ☐ Dump Station   ☐ Composting   ☐ No

☐ Sewer   ☐ Water Pressure ☺ ☹   ☐ Flush

Security

☐ Attendant - Hours _____   ☐ Gates

☐ Camp Host - Hours _____   Lock Out Times _____

Opening_____   Closing_____

Connectivity   Signal Quality (circle one)

☐ WiFi   ☐ Free   ☐ Fee _____

☐ Cell Service   Carrier _____

☐ TV   ☐ Free   ☐ Fee _____

Facilities

☐ Laundry   Cost _____   ☐ Gym   ☐ Free   ☐ Fee _____

☐ Pool   ☐ Hot Tub   ☐ Club House ☐ Free   ☐ Fee _____

☐ Boating   ☐ Pet Friendly - ☐ Free ☐ Fee _____

Food Options   Kids Activities

☐ Groceries   ☐ Restaurants   ☐ Playground   ☐ Parks

☐ Snack Bar   ☐ Other Shops

Local Highlights

Things to do/Recommendations

Rating (choose 1 to 5 🔥)

🔥 🔥 🔥 🔥 🔥

Notes

Campground Name _____

Address _____

Website _____ Email _____

Phone _____ Hours _____

Category

☐ National Park   ☐ County Park   ☐ Private   ☐ Army Corp. of Eng.

☐ State Park   ☐ BLM   ☐ Province/Parish ☐ Other _____

Rates ($, £ , €) (circle one)

Daily _____ Monthly _____

Weekly _____ Long Stay _____

Services   Toilets   Showers

☐ Electric   Amp_____   ☐ Pit   ☐ None   ☐ Yes

☐ Water   ☐ Dump Station   ☐ Composting   ☐ No

☐ Sewer   ☐ Water Pressure ☺ ☹   ☐ Flush

Security

☐ Attendant - Hours _____   ☐ Gates

☐ Camp Host - Hours _____   Lock Out Times _____

                                        Opening _____ Closing _____

Connectivity   Signal Quality (circle one)

☐ WiFi   ☐ Free   ☐ Fee _____

☐ Cell Service   Carrier _____

☐ TV   ☐ Free   ☐ Fee _____

Facilities

☐ Laundry   Cost _____   ☐ Gym   ☐ Free   ☐ Fee _____

☐ Pool   ☐ Hot Tub   ☐ Club House   ☐ Free   ☐ Fee _____

☐ Boating   ☐ Pet Friendly - ☐ Free   ☐ Fee _____

Food Options   ## Kids Activities

☐ Groceries   ☐ Restaurants   ☐ Playground   ☐ Parks

☐ Snack Bar   ☐ Other Shops

Local Highlights

Things to do/Recommendations

Rating (choose 1 to 5 🔥)

Notes

Campground Name _____

Address _____

Website _____ Email _____

Phone _____ Hours _____

Category

- ☐ National Park
- ☐ County Park
- ☐ Private
- ☐ Army Corp. of Eng.
- ☐ State Park
- ☐ BLM
- ☐ Province/Parish
- ☐ Other _____

Rates ($, £ , €) (circle one)

Daily _____ Monthly _____

Weekly _____ Long Stay _____

Services

- ☐ Electric   Amp_____
- ☐ Water   ☐ Dump Station
- ☐ Sewer   ☐ Water Pressure ☺ ☹

Toilets

- ☐ Pit
- ☐ Composting
- ☐ Flush

Showers

- ☐ None ☐ Yes
- ☐ No

Security

- ☐ Attendant - Hours _____
- ☐ Camp Host - Hours _____
- ☐ Gates
- Lock Out Times _____
- Opening _____ Closing _____

Connectivity

- ☐ WiFi   ☐ Free   ☐ Fee _____
- ☐ Cell Service   Carrier _____
- ☐ TV   ☐ Free   ☐ Fee _____

Signal Quality (circle one)

Facilities

- ☐ Laundry   Cost _____
- ☐ Pool   ☐ Hot Tub
- ☐ Boating   ☐ Pet Friendly - ☐ Free ☐ Fee _____
- ☐ Gym   ☐ Free ☐ Fee _____
- ☐ Club House ☐ Free ☐ Fee _____

Food Options

- ☐ Groceries   ☐ Restaurants
- ☐ Snack Bar   ☐ Other Shops

Kids Activities

- ☐ Playground   ☐ Parks

Local Highlights

Things to do/Recommendations

Rating (choose 1 to 5 🔥)

🔥 🔥 🔥 🔥 🔥

Notes

Campground Name _____

Address _____

Website _____ Email _____

Phone _____ Hours _____

Category

- ☐ National Park
- ☐ County Park
- ☐ Private
- ☐ Army Corp. of Eng.
- ☐ State Park
- ☐ BLM
- ☐ Province/Parish
- ☐ Other _____

Rates ($, £ , €) (circle one)

Daily _____ Monthly _____

Weekly _____ Long Stay _____

Services | Toilets | Showers

- ☐ Electric   Amp _____   ☐ Pit   ☐ None   ☐ Yes
- ☐ Water   ☐ Dump Station   ☐ Composting   ☐ No
- ☐ Sewer   ☐ Water Pressure ☺ ☹   ☐ Flush

Security

- ☐ Attendant - Hours _____   ☐ Gates
- ☐ Camp Host - Hours _____   Lock Out Times _____
- Opening _____   Closing _____

Connectivity | Signal Quality (circle one)

- ☐ WiFi   ☐ Free   ☐ Fee _____
- ☐ Cell Service   Carrier _____
- ☐ TV   ☐ Free   ☐ Fee _____

Facilities

- ☐ Laundry   Cost _____   ☐ Gym   ☐ Free   ☐ Fee _____
- ☐ Pool   ☐ Hot Tub   ☐ Club House   ☐ Free   ☐ Fee _____
- ☐ Boating   ☐ Pet Friendly -   ☐ Free   ☐ Fee _____

Food Options | Kids Activities

- ☐ Groceries   ☐ Restaurants   ☐ Playground   ☐ Parks
- ☐ Snack Bar   ☐ Other Shops

Local Highlights

Things to do/Recommendations

Rating (choose 1 to 5 🔥)

🔥 🔥 🔥 🔥 🔥

Notes

Campground Name _____

Address _____

Website _____   Email _____

Phone _____   Hours _____

Category

- ☐ National Park
- ☐ County Park
- ☐ Private
- ☐ Army Corp. of Eng.
- ☐ State Park
- ☐ BLM
- ☐ Province/Parish
- ☐ Other _____

Rates ($, £ , €) (circle one)

Daily _____   Monthly _____

Weekly _____   Long Stay _____

Services   Toilets   Showers

- ☐ Electric   Amp_____
- ☐ Pit   ☐ None   ☐ Yes
- ☐ Water   ☐ Dump Station
- ☐ Composting   ☐ No
- ☐ Sewer   ☐ Water Pressure ☺ ☹
- ☐ Flush

Security

- ☐ Attendant - Hours _____
- ☐ Gates
- ☐ Camp Host - Hours _____

Lock Out Times _____

Opening _____   Closing _____

Connectivity   Signal Quality (circle one)

- ☐ WiFi   ☐ Free   ☐ Fee _____
- ☐ Cell Service   Carrier _____
- ☐ TV   ☐ Free   ☐ Fee _____

Facilities

- ☐ Laundry   Cost _____
- ☐ Gym   ☐ Free   ☐ Fee _____
- ☐ Pool   ☐ Hot Tub
- ☐ Club House   ☐ Free   ☐ Fee _____
- ☐ Boating   ☐ Pet Friendly -   ☐ Free   ☐ Fee _____

Food Options   Kids Activities

- ☐ Groceries   ☐ Restaurants
- ☐ Playground   ☐ Parks
- ☐ Snack Bar   ☐ Other Shops

Local Highlights

Things to do/Recommendations

Rating (choose 1 to 5 🔥)

🔥 🔥 🔥 🔥 🔥 🔥

Notes

Campground Name _____

Address _____

Website _____ Email _____

Phone _____ Hours _____

Category

- ☐ National Park
- ☐ County Park
- ☐ Private
- ☐ Army Corp. of Eng.
- ☐ State Park
- ☐ BLM
- ☐ Province/Parish
- ☐ Other _____

Rates ($, £ , €) (circle one)

Daily _____ Monthly _____

Weekly _____ Long Stay _____

Services

- ☐ Electric   Amp _____
- ☐ Water   ☐ Dump Station
- ☐ Sewer   ☐ Water Pressure ☺ ☹

Toilets

- ☐ Pit
- ☐ None
- ☐ Composting
- ☐ Flush

Showers

- ☐ Yes
- ☐ No

Security

- ☐ Attendant - Hours _____
- ☐ Camp Host - Hours _____
- ☐ Gates

Lock Out Times _____

Opening _____ Closing _____

Connectivity

- ☐ WiFi   ☐ Free   ☐ Fee _____
- ☐ Cell Service   Carrier _____
- ☐ TV   ☐ Free   ☐ Fee _____

Signal Quality (circle one)

Facilities

- ☐ Laundry   Cost _____
- ☐ Pool   ☐ Hot Tub
- ☐ Boating   ☐ Pet Friendly -   ☐ Free   ☐ Fee _____
- ☐ Gym   ☐ Free   ☐ Fee _____
- ☐ Club House   ☐ Free   ☐ Fee _____

Food Options

- ☐ Groceries   ☐ Restaurants
- ☐ Snack Bar   ☐ Other Shops

Kids Activities

- ☐ Playground   ☐ Parks

Local Highlights

Things to do/Recommendations

Rating (choose 1 to 5 🔥)

🔥 🔥 🔥 🔥 🔥

Notes

Campground Name _____

Address _____

Website _____   Email _____

Phone _____   Hours _____

Category

- ☐ National Park
- ☐ County Park
- ☐ Private
- ☐ Army Corp. of Eng.
- ☐ State Park
- ☐ BLM
- ☐ Province/Parish
- ☐ Other _____

Rates ($, £ , €) (circle one)

Daily _____   Monthly _____

Weekly _____   Long Stay _____

Services   Toilets   Showers

- ☐ Electric   Amp_____   ☐ Pit   ☐ None   ☐ Yes
- ☐ Water   ☐ Dump Station   ☐ Composting   ☐ No
- ☐ Sewer   ☐ Water Pressure ☺ ☹   ☐ Flush

Security

- ☐ Attendant - Hours _____   ☐ Gates
- ☐ Camp Host - Hours _____   Lock Out Times _____

  Opening _____   Closing _____

Connectivity   Signal Quality (circle one)

- ☐ WiFi   ☐ Free   ☐ Fee _____
- ☐ Cell Service   Carrier _____
- ☐ TV   ☐ Free   ☐ Fee _____

Facilities

- ☐ Laundry   Cost _____   ☐ Gym   ☐ Free   ☐ Fee _____
- ☐ Pool   ☐ Hot Tub   ☐ Club House ☐ Free   ☐ Fee _____
- ☐ Boating   ☐ Pet Friendly - ☐ Free ☐ Fee _____

Food Options   Kids Activities

- ☐ Groceries   ☐ Restaurants   ☐ Playground   ☐ Parks
- ☐ Snack Bar   ☐ Other Shops

Local Highlights

Things to do/Recommendations

Rating (choose 1 to 5 🔥)

🔥 🔥 🔥 🔥 🔥

Notes

Campground Name _____

Address _____

Website _____ Email _____

Phone _____ Hours _____

Category

- ☐ National Park
- ☐ County Park
- ☐ Private
- ☐ Army Corp. of Eng.
- ☐ State Park
- ☐ BLM
- ☐ Province/Parish
- ☐ Other _____

Rates ($, £ , €) (circle one)

Daily _____ Monthly _____

Weekly _____ Long Stay _____

Services   Toilets   Showers

- ☐ Electric   Amp_____   ☐ Pit   ☐ None   ☐ Yes
- ☐ Water   ☐ Dump Station   ☐ Composting   ☐ No
- ☐ Sewer   ☐ Water Pressure ☺ ☹   ☐ Flush

Security

- ☐ Attendant - Hours _____   ☐ Gates
- ☐ Camp Host - Hours _____   Lock Out Times _____
  Opening _____   Closing _____

Connectivity   Signal Quality (circle one)

- ☐ WiFi   ☐ Free   ☐ Fee _____
- ☐ Cell Service   Carrier _____
- ☐ TV   ☐ Free   ☐ Fee _____

Facilities

- ☐ Laundry   Cost _____   ☐ Gym   ☐ Free   ☐ Fee _____
- ☐ Pool   ☐ Hot Tub   ☐ Club House   ☐ Free   ☐ Fee _____
- ☐ Boating   ☐ Pet Friendly -   ☐ Free   ☐ Fee _____

Food Options   Kids Activities

- ☐ Groceries   ☐ Restaurants   ☐ Playground   ☐ Parks
- ☐ Snack Bar   ☐ Other Shops

Local Highlights

Things to do/Recommendations

Rating (choose 1 to 5 🔥)

🔥 🔥 🔥 🔥 🔥

Notes

Campground Name _____

Address _____

Website _____ Email _____

Phone _____ Hours _____

Category

- ☐ National Park
- ☐ County Park
- ☐ Private
- ☐ Army Corp. of Eng.
- ☐ State Park
- ☐ BLM
- ☐ Province/Parish
- ☐ Other _____

Rates ($, £ , €) (circle one)

Daily _____ Monthly _____

Weekly _____ Long Stay _____

Services   Toilets   Showers

- ☐ Electric   Amp _____
- ☐ Pit   ☐ None   ☐ Yes
- ☐ Water   ☐ Dump Station
- ☐ Composting   ☐ No
- ☐ Sewer   ☐ Water Pressure ☺ ☹
- ☐ Flush

Security

- ☐ Attendant - Hours _____
- ☐ Gates
- ☐ Camp Host - Hours _____
- Lock Out Times _____
- Opening _____ Closing _____

Connectivity   Signal Quality (circle one)

- ☐ WiFi   ☐ Free   ☐ Fee _____
- ☐ Cell Service   Carrier _____
- ☐ TV   ☐ Free   ☐ Fee _____

Facilities

- ☐ Laundry   Cost _____
- ☐ Gym   ☐ Free   ☐ Fee _____
- ☐ Pool   ☐ Hot Tub
- ☐ Club House ☐ Free   ☐ Fee _____
- ☐ Boating   ☐ Pet Friendly - ☐ Free ☐ Fee _____

Food Options   Kids Activities

- ☐ Groceries   ☐ Restaurants
- ☐ Playground ☐ Parks
- ☐ Snack Bar   ☐ Other Shops

Local Highlights

Things to do/Recommendations

Rating (choose 1 to 5 🔥)

🔥 🔥 🔥 🔥 🔥

Notes

Campground Name _____

Address _____

Website _____ Email _____

Phone _____ Hours _____

Category

☐ National Park   ☐ County Park   ☐ Private   ☐ Army Corp. of Eng.

☐ State Park   ☐ BLM   ☐ Province/Parish   ☐ Other _____

Rates ($, £ , €) (circle one)

Daily _____ Monthly _____

Weekly _____ Long Stay _____

Services   Toilets   Showers

☐ Electric   Amp_____   ☐ Pit   ☐ None   ☐ Yes

☐ Water   ☐ Dump Station   ☐ Composting   ☐ No

☐ Sewer   ☐ Water Pressure ☺ ☹   ☐ Flush

Security

☐ Attendant - Hours_____   ☐ Gates

☐ Camp Host - Hours_____   Lock Out Times _____

Opening_____   Closing_____

Connectivity   Signal Quality (circle one)

☐ WiFi   ☐ Free   ☐ Fee _____

☐ Cell Service Carrier _____

☐ TV   ☐ Free   ☐ Fee _____

Facilities

☐ Laundry   Cost _____   ☐ Gym   ☐ Free   ☐ Fee _____

☐ Pool   ☐ Hot Tub   ☐ Club House ☐ Free   ☐ Fee _____

☐ Boating   ☐ Pet Friendly - ☐ Free   ☐ Fee _____

Food Options   Kids Activities

☐ Groceries   ☐ Restaurants   ☐ Playground   ☐ Parks

☐ Snack Bar   ☐ Other Shops

Local Highlights

Things to do/Recommendations

Rating (choose 1 to 5 🔥)

Notes

Campground Name _____

Address _____

Website _____ Email _____

Phone _____ Hours _____

Category

☐ National Park ☐ County Park ☐ Private ☐ Army Corp. of Eng.

☐ State Park ☐ BLM ☐ Province/Parish ☐ Other _____

Rates ($, £ , €) (circle one)

Daily _____ Monthly _____

Weekly _____ Long Stay _____

Services   Toilets   Showers

☐ Electric   Amp_____   ☐ Pit   ☐ None   ☐ Yes

☐ Water   ☐ Dump Station   ☐ Composting   ☐ No

☐ Sewer   ☐ Water Pressure ☺ ☹   ☐ Flush

Security

☐ Attendant - Hours _____   ☐ Gates

☐ Camp Host - Hours _____   Lock Out Times _____

Opening _____   Closing _____

Connectivity   Signal Quality (circle one)

☐ WiFi   ☐ Free   ☐ Fee _____

☐ Cell Service   Carrier _____

☐ TV   ☐ Free   ☐ Fee _____

Facilities

☐ Laundry   Cost _____   ☐ Gym   ☐ Free   ☐ Fee _____

☐ Pool   ☐ Hot Tub   ☐ Club House   ☐ Free   ☐ Fee _____

☐ Boating   ☐ Pet Friendly - ☐ Free   ☐ Fee _____

Food Options   Kids Activities

☐ Groceries   ☐ Restaurants   ☐ Playground   ☐ Parks

☐ Snack Bar   ☐ Other Shops

Local Highlights

Things to do/Recommendations

Rating (choose 1 to 5 🔥)

🔥 🔥 🔥 🔥 🔥

Notes

Campground Name _____

Address _____

Website _____ Email _____

Phone _____ Hours _____

Category

- ☐ National Park
- ☐ County Park
- ☐ Private
- ☐ Army Corp. of Eng.
- ☐ State Park
- ☐ BLM
- ☐ Province/Parish
- ☐ Other _____

Rates ($, £ , €) (circle one)

Daily _____ Monthly _____

Weekly _____ Long Stay _____

Services

- ☐ Electric   Amp_____
- ☐ Water   ☐ Dump Station
- ☐ Sewer   ☐ Water Pressure ☺ ☹

Toilets

- ☐ Pit
- ☐ Composting
- ☐ Flush

Showers

- ☐ None ☐ Yes
- ☐ No

Security

- ☐ Attendant - Hours _____
- ☐ Camp Host - Hours _____
- ☐ Gates
- Lock Out Times _____
- Opening _____ Closing _____

Connectivity

- ☐ WiFi   ☐ Free   ☐ Fee _____
- ☐ Cell Service   Carrier _____
- ☐ TV   ☐ Free   ☐ Fee _____

Signal Quality (circle one)

Facilities

- ☐ Laundry   Cost _____   ☐ Gym   ☐ Free   ☐ Fee _____
- ☐ Pool   ☐ Hot Tub   ☐ Club House   ☐ Free   ☐ Fee _____
- ☐ Boating   ☐ Pet Friendly -   ☐ Free   ☐ Fee _____

Food Options

- ☐ Groceries   ☐ Restaurants
- ☐ Snack Bar   ☐ Other Shops

Kids Activities

- ☐ Playground   ☐ Parks

Local Highlights

Things to do/Recommendations

Rating (choose 1 to 5 🔥)

🔥 🔥 🔥 🔥 🔥

Notes

Campground Name _____

Address _____

Website _____ Email _____

Phone _____ Hours _____

Category

- ☐ National Park
- ☐ County Park
- ☐ Private
- ☐ Army Corp. of Eng.
- ☐ State Park
- ☐ BLM
- ☐ Province/Parish
- ☐ Other _____

Rates ($, £ , €) (circle one)

Daily _____ Monthly _____

Weekly _____ Long Stay _____

Services | Toilets | Showers

- ☐ Electric   Amp_____
- ☐ Water   ☐ Dump Station
- ☐ Sewer   ☐ Water Pressure ☺ ☹

- ☐ Pit   ☐ None   ☐ Yes
- ☐ Composting   ☐ No
- ☐ Flush

Security

- ☐ Attendant - Hours _____
- ☐ Camp Host - Hours _____
- ☐ Gates
- Lock Out Times _____
- Opening _____ Closing _____

Connectivity

Signal Quality (circle one)

- ☐ WiFi   ☐ Free   ☐ Fee _____
- ☐ Cell Service   Carrier _____
- ☐ TV   ☐ Free   ☐ Fee _____

Facilities

- ☐ Laundry   Cost _____
- ☐ Pool   ☐ Hot Tub
- ☐ Boating   ☐ Pet Friendly - ☐ Free ☐ Fee _____
- ☐ Gym   ☐ Free   ☐ Fee _____
- ☐ Club House ☐ Free   ☐ Fee _____

Food Options | Kids Activities

- ☐ Groceries   ☐ Restaurants
- ☐ Snack Bar   ☐ Other Shops
- ☐ Playground   ☐ Parks

Local Highlights

Things to do/Recommendations

Rating (choose 1 to 5 🔥)

🔥 🔥 🔥 🔥 🔥 🔥

Notes

Campground Name _____

Address _____

Website _____ Email _____

Phone _____ Hours _____

Category

- ☐ National Park
- ☐ County Park
- ☐ Private
- ☐ Army Corp. of Eng.
- ☐ State Park
- ☐ BLM
- ☐ Province/Parish
- ☐ Other _____

Rates ($, £ , €) (circle one)

Daily _____ Monthly _____

Weekly _____ Long Stay _____

Services   Toilets   Showers

- ☐ Electric   Amp_____   ☐ Pit   ☐ None   ☐ Yes
- ☐ Water   ☐ Dump Station   ☐ Composting   ☐ No
- ☐ Sewer   ☐ Water Pressure ☺ ☹ ☐ Flush

Security

- ☐ Attendant - Hours _____   ☐ Gates
- ☐ Camp Host - Hours _____   Lock Out Times _____

  Opening _____   Closing _____

Connectivity   Signal Quality (circle one)

- ☐ WiFi   ☐ Free   ☐ Fee _____
- ☐ Cell Service   Carrier _____
- ☐ TV   ☐ Free   ☐ Fee _____

Facilities

- ☐ Laundry   Cost _____   ☐ Gym   ☐ Free   ☐ Fee _____
- ☐ Pool   ☐ Hot Tub   ☐ Club House ☐ Free   ☐ Fee _____
- ☐ Boating   ☐ Pet Friendly - ☐ Free ☐ Fee _____

Food Options   Kids Activities

- ☐ Groceries   ☐ Restaurants   ☐ Playground   ☐ Parks
- ☐ Snack Bar   ☐ Other Shops

Local Highlights

Things to do/Recommendations

Rating (choose 1 to 5 🔥)

🔥 🔥 🔥 🔥 🔥

Notes

Campground Name _____

Address _____

Website _____ Email _____

Phone _____ Hours _____

Category

☐ National Park   ☐ County Park   ☐ Private   ☐ Army Corp. of Eng.

☐ State Park   ☐ BLM   ☐ Province/Parish   ☐ Other _____

Rates ($, £ , €) (circle one)

Daily _____ Monthly _____

Weekly _____ Long Stay _____

Services   Toilets   Showers

☐ Electric   Amp_____   ☐ Pit   ☐ None   ☐ Yes

☐ Water   ☐ Dump Station   ☐ Composting   ☐ No

☐ Sewer   ☐ Water Pressure ☺ ☹   ☐ Flush

Security

☐ Attendant - Hours_____   ☐ Gates

☐ Camp Host - Hours_____   Lock Out Times _____

Opening _____   Closing _____

Connectivity   Signal Quality (circle one)

☐ WiFi   ☐ Free   ☐ Fee _____

☐ Cell Service   Carrier _____

☐ TV   ☐ Free   ☐ Fee _____

Facilities

☐ Laundry   Cost _____   ☐ Gym   ☐ Free   ☐ Fee _____

☐ Pool   ☐ Hot Tub   ☐ Club House   ☐ Free   ☐ Fee _____

☐ Boating   ☐ Pet Friendly -   ☐ Free   ☐ Fee _____

Food Options   Kids Activities

☐ Groceries   ☐ Restaurants   ☐ Playground   ☐ Parks

☐ Snack Bar   ☐ Other Shops

Local Highlights

Things to do/Recommendations

Rating (choose 1 to 5 🔥)

🔥 🔥 🔥 🔥 🔥 🔥

Notes

Campground Name _____

Address _____

Website _____ Email _____

Phone _____ Hours _____

Category

☐ National Park   ☐ County Park   ☐ Private   ☐ Army Corp. of Eng.

☐ State Park   ☐ BLM   ☐ Province/Parish   ☐ Other _____

Rates ($, £ , €) (circle one)

Daily _____   Monthly _____

Weekly _____   Long Stay _____

Services   Toilets   Showers

☐ Electric   Amp _____   ☐ Pit   ☐ None   ☐ Yes

☐ Water   ☐ Dump Station   ☐ Composting   ☐ No

☐ Sewer   ☐ Water Pressure ☺ ☹   ☐ Flush

Security

☐ Attendant - Hours _____   ☐ Gates

☐ Camp Host - Hours _____   Lock Out Times _____

                                         Opening _____   Closing _____

Connectivity   Signal Quality (circle one)

☐ WiFi   ☐ Free   ☐ Fee _____

☐ Cell Service   Carrier _____

☐ TV   ☐ Free   ☐ Fee _____

Facilities

☐ Laundry   Cost _____   ☐ Gym   ☐ Free   ☐ Fee _____

☐ Pool   ☐ Hot Tub   ☐ Club House   ☐ Free   ☐ Fee _____

☐ Boating   ☐ Pet Friendly - ☐ Free   ☐ Fee _____

Food Options   ## Kids Activities

☐ Groceries   ☐ Restaurants   ☐ Playground   ☐ Parks

☐ Snack Bar   ☐ Other Shops

Local Highlights

Things to do/Recommendations

Rating (choose 1 to 5 🔥)

Notes

Campground Name _____

Address _____

Website _____ Email _____

Phone _____ Hours _____

Category

☐ National Park   ☐ County Park   ☐ Private   ☐ Army Corp. of Eng.

☐ State Park   ☐ BLM   ☐ Province/Parish   ☐ Other _____

Rates ($, £ , €) (circle one)

Daily _____ Monthly _____

Weekly _____ Long Stay _____

Services   Toilets   Showers

☐ Electric   Amp_____   ☐ Pit   ☐ None   ☐ Yes

☐ Water   ☐ Dump Station   ☐ Composting   ☐ No

☐ Sewer   ☐ Water Pressure ☺ ☹   ☐ Flush

Security

☐ Attendant - Hours_____   ☐ Gates

☐ Camp Host - Hours_____   Lock Out Times _____

Opening_____   Closing_____

Connectivity   Signal Quality (circle one)

☐ WiFi   ☐ Free   ☐ Fee _____

☐ Cell Service   Carrier _____

☐ TV   ☐ Free   ☐ Fee _____

Facilities

☐ Laundry   Cost _____   ☐ Gym   ☐ Free   ☐ Fee _____

☐ Pool   ☐ Hot Tub   ☐ Club House   ☐ Free   ☐ Fee _____

☐ Boating   ☐ Pet Friendly - ☐ Free ☐ Fee _____

Food Options   Kids Activities

☐ Groceries   ☐ Restaurants   ☐ Playground   ☐ Parks

☐ Snack Bar   ☐ Other Shops

Local Highlights

Things to do/Recommendations

Rating (choose 1 to 5 🔥)

🔥 🔥 🔥 🔥 🔥

Notes

Campground Name _____

Address _____

Website _____ Email _____

Phone _____ Hours _____

Category

- ☐ National Park
- ☐ County Park
- ☐ Private
- ☐ Army Corp. of Eng.
- ☐ State Park
- ☐ BLM
- ☐ Province/Parish
- ☐ Other _____

Rates ($, £ , €) (circle one)

Daily _____ Monthly _____

Weekly _____ Long Stay _____

Services

- ☐ Electric   Amp_____
- ☐ Water   ☐ Dump Station
- ☐ Sewer   ☐ Water Pressure ☺ ☹

Toilets

- ☐ Pit
- ☐ Composting
- ☐ Flush

Showers

- ☐ None   ☐ Yes
- ☐ No

Security

- ☐ Attendant - Hours _____
- ☐ Camp Host - Hours _____
- ☐ Gates
- Lock Out Times _____
- Opening _____   Closing _____

Connectivity

- ☐ WiFi   ☐ Free   ☐ Fee _____
- ☐ Cell Service   Carrier _____
- ☐ TV   ☐ Free   ☐ Fee _____

Signal Quality (circle one)

Facilities

- ☐ Laundry   Cost _____
- ☐ Pool   ☐ Hot Tub
- ☐ Boating   ☐ Pet Friendly - ☐ Free ☐ Fee _____
- ☐ Gym   ☐ Free   ☐ Fee _____
- ☐ Club House ☐ Free   ☐ Fee _____

Food Options

- ☐ Groceries   ☐ Restaurants
- ☐ Snack Bar   ☐ Other Shops

Kids Activities

- ☐ Playground   ☐ Parks

Local Highlights

Things to do/Recommendations

Rating (choose 1 to 5 🔥)

🔥 🔥 🔥 🔥 🔥

Notes

Campground Name _____

Address _____

Website _____ Email _____

Phone _____ Hours _____

Category

- ☐ National Park
- ☐ County Park
- ☐ Private
- ☐ Army Corp. of Eng.
- ☐ State Park
- ☐ BLM
- ☐ Province/Parish
- ☐ Other _____

Rates ($, £ , €) (circle one)

Daily _____ Monthly _____

Weekly _____ Long Stay _____

Services

- ☐ Electric   Amp_____
- ☐ Water   ☐ Dump Station
- ☐ Sewer   ☐ Water Pressure 🙂 🙁

Toilets

- ☐ Pit
- ☐ Composting
- ☐ Flush
- ☐ None

Showers

- ☐ Yes
- ☐ No

Security

- ☐ Attendant - Hours _____
- ☐ Camp Host - Hours _____
- ☐ Gates
- Lock Out Times _____
- Opening _____   Closing _____

Connectivity

- ☐ WiFi   ☐ Free   ☐ Fee _____
- ☐ Cell Service   Carrier _____
- ☐ TV   ☐ Free   ☐ Fee _____

Signal Quality (circle one)

Facilities

- ☐ Laundry   Cost _____
- ☐ Pool   ☐ Hot Tub
- ☐ Boating   ☐ Pet Friendly - ☐ Free ☐ Fee _____
- ☐ Gym   ☐ Free   ☐ Fee _____
- ☐ Club House   ☐ Free   ☐ Fee _____

Food Options

- ☐ Groceries   ☐ Restaurants
- ☐ Snack Bar   ☐ Other Shops

Kids Activities

- ☐ Playground   ☐ Parks

Local Highlights

Things to do/Recommendations

Rating (choose 1 to 5 🔥)

🔥 🔥 🔥 🔥 🔥

Notes

Campground Name _____

Address _____

Website _____ Email _____

Phone _____ Hours _____

Category

- ☐ National Park
- ☐ County Park
- ☐ Private
- ☐ Army Corp. of Eng.
- ☐ State Park
- ☐ BLM
- ☐ Province/Parish
- ☐ Other _____

Rates ($, £ , €) (circle one)

Daily _____ Monthly _____

Weekly _____ Long Stay _____

Services

- ☐ Electric   Amp_____
- ☐ Water   ☐ Dump Station
- ☐ Sewer   ☐ Water Pressure ☺ ☹

Toilets

- ☐ Pit
- ☐ None
- ☐ Composting
- ☐ Flush

Showers

- ☐ Yes
- ☐ No

Security

- ☐ Attendant - Hours _____
- ☐ Camp Host - Hours _____
- ☐ Gates
- Lock Out Times _____
- Opening _____ Closing _____

Connectivity

- ☐ WiFi   ☐ Free   ☐ Fee _____
- ☐ Cell Service   Carrier _____
- ☐ TV   ☐ Free   ☐ Fee _____

Signal Quality (circle one)

Facilities

- ☐ Laundry   Cost _____
- ☐ Pool   ☐ Hot Tub
- ☐ Boating   ☐ Pet Friendly - ☐ Free ☐ Fee _____
- ☐ Gym   ☐ Free   ☐ Fee _____
- ☐ Club House   ☐ Free   ☐ Fee _____

Food Options

- ☐ Groceries   ☐ Restaurants
- ☐ Snack Bar   ☐ Other Shops

Kids Activities

- ☐ Playground   ☐ Parks

Local Highlights

Things to do/Recommendations

Rating (choose 1 to 5 🔥)

🔥 🔥 🔥 🔥 🔥

Notes

Campground Name _____

Address _____

Website _____   Email _____

Phone _____   Hours _____

Category

☐ National Park   ☐ County Park   ☐ Private   ☐ Army Corp. of Eng.

☐ State Park   ☐ BLM   ☐ Province/Parish   ☐ Other _____

Rates ($, £ , €) (circle one)

Daily _____   Monthly _____

Weekly _____   Long Stay _____

Services   Toilets   Showers

☐ Electric   Amp _____   ☐ Pit   ☐ None   ☐ Yes

☐ Water   ☐ Dump Station   ☐ Composting   ☐ No

☐ Sewer   ☐ Water Pressure ☺ ☹   ☐ Flush

Security

☐ Attendant - Hours _____   ☐ Gates

☐ Camp Host - Hours _____   Lock Out Times _____

Opening _____   Closing _____

Connectivity   Signal Quality (circle one)

☐ WiFi   ☐ Free   ☐ Fee _____

☐ Cell Service   Carrier _____

☐ TV   ☐ Free   ☐ Fee _____

Facilities

☐ Laundry   Cost _____   ☐ Gym   ☐ Free   ☐ Fee _____

☐ Pool   ☐ Hot Tub   ☐ Club House   ☐ Free   ☐ Fee _____

☐ Boating   ☐ Pet Friendly - ☐ Free ☐ Fee _____

Food Options   Kids Activities

☐ Groceries   ☐ Restaurants   ☐ Playground   ☐ Parks

☐ Snack Bar   ☐ Other Shops

Local Highlights

Things to do/Recommendations

Rating (choose 1 to 5 🔥)

🔥 🔥 🔥 🔥 🔥 🔥

Notes

Campground Name _____

Address _____

Website _____   Email _____

Phone _____   Hours _____

Category

☐ National Park   ☐ County Park   ☐ Private   ☐ Army Corp. of Eng.

☐ State Park   ☐ BLM   ☐ Province/Parish   ☐ Other _____

Rates ($, £ , €) (circle one)

Daily _____   Monthly _____

Weekly _____   Long Stay _____

Services   Toilets   Showers

☐ Electric   Amp _____   ☐ Pit   ☐ None   ☐ Yes

☐ Water   ☐ Dump Station   ☐ Composting   ☐ No

☐ Sewer   ☐ Water Pressure ☺ ☹   ☐ Flush

Security

☐ Attendant - Hours _____   ☐ Gates

☐ Camp Host - Hours _____   Lock Out Times _____

Opening _____   Closing _____

Connectivity   Signal Quality (circle one)

☐ WiFi   ☐ Free   ☐ Fee _____

☐ Cell Service   Carrier _____

☐ TV   ☐ Free   ☐ Fee _____

Facilities

☐ Laundry   Cost _____   ☐ Gym   ☐ Free   ☐ Fee _____

☐ Pool   ☐ Hot Tub   ☐ Club House   ☐ Free   ☐ Fee _____

☐ Boating   ☐ Pet Friendly - ☐ Free ☐ Fee _____

Food Options   Kids Activities

☐ Groceries   ☐ Restaurants   ☐ Playground   ☐ Parks

☐ Snack Bar   ☐ Other Shops

Local Highlights

Things to do/Recommendations

Rating (choose 1 to 5 🔥)

🔥 🔥 🔥 🔥 🔥

Notes

Campground Name _____

Address _____

Website _____ Email _____

Phone _____ Hours _____

Category

☐ National Park ☐ County Park ☐ Private ☐ Army Corp. of Eng.

☐ State Park ☐ BLM ☐ Province/Parish ☐ Other _____

Rates ($, £ , €) (circle one)

Daily _____ Monthly _____

Weekly _____ Long Stay _____

Services	Toilets	Showers
☐ Electric Amp_____	☐ Pit ☐ None	☐ Yes
☐ Water ☐ Dump Station	☐ Composting	☐ No
☐ Sewer ☐ Water Pressure ☺ ☹	☐ Flush	

Security

☐ Attendant - Hours _____ ☐ Gates

☐ Camp Host - Hours _____ Lock Out Times _____

Opening _____   Closing _____

Connectivity

Signal Quality (circle one)

☐ WiFi   ☐ Free   ☐ Fee _____

☐ Cell Service   Carrier _____

☐ TV   ☐ Free   ☐ Fee _____

Facilities

☐ Laundry   Cost _____   ☐ Gym   ☐ Free   ☐ Fee _____

☐ Pool   ☐ Hot Tub   ☐ Club House   ☐ Free   ☐ Fee _____

☐ Boating   ☐ Pet Friendly - ☐ Free   ☐ Fee _____

Food Options

Kids Activities

☐ Groceries   ☐ Restaurants   ☐ Playground   ☐ Parks

☐ Snack Bar   ☐ Other Shops

Local Highlights

Things to do/Recommendations

Rating (choose 1 to 5 🔥)

🔥 🔥 🔥 🔥 🔥

Notes

Campground Name _____

Address _____

Website _____ Email _____

Phone _____ Hours _____

Category

☐ National Park   ☐ County Park   ☐ Private   ☐ Army Corp. of Eng.

☐ State Park   ☐ BLM   ☐ Province/Parish   ☐ Other _____

Rates ($, £ , €) (circle one)

Daily _____   Monthly _____

Weekly _____   Long Stay _____

Services   Toilets   Showers

☐ Electric   Amp_____   ☐ Pit   ☐ None   ☐ Yes

☐ Water   ☐ Dump Station   ☐ Composting   ☐ No

☐ Sewer   ☐ Water Pressure ☺ ☹   ☐ Flush

Security

☐ Attendant - Hours _____   ☐ Gates

☐ Camp Host - Hours _____   Lock Out Times _____

                                        Opening _____   Closing _____

Connectivity   Signal Quality (circle one)

☐ WiFi   ☐ Free   ☐ Fee _____

☐ Cell Service   Carrier _____

☐ TV   ☐ Free   ☐ Fee _____

Facilities

☐ Laundry   Cost _____   ☐ Gym   ☐ Free   ☐ Fee _____

☐ Pool   ☐ Hot Tub   ☐ Club House   ☐ Free   ☐ Fee _____

☐ Boating   ☐ Pet Friendly -   ☐ Free   ☐ Fee _____

Food Options   Kids Activities

☐ Groceries   ☐ Restaurants   ☐ Playground   ☐ Parks

☐ Snack Bar   ☐ Other Shops

Local Highlights

Things to do/Recommendations

Rating (choose 1 to 5 🔥)

Notes

Campground Name _____

Address _____

Website _____ Email _____

Phone _____ Hours _____

Category

- ☐ National Park
- ☐ County Park
- ☐ Private
- ☐ Army Corp. of Eng.
- ☐ State Park
- ☐ BLM
- ☐ Province/Parish
- ☐ Other _____

Rates ($, £ , €) (circle one)

Daily _____   Monthly _____

Weekly _____   Long Stay _____

Services | Toilets | Showers

- ☐ Electric Amp _____
- ☐ Water   ☐ Dump Station
- ☐ Sewer   ☐ Water Pressure ☺ ☹

- ☐ Pit   ☐ None
- ☐ Composting
- ☐ Flush

- ☐ Yes
- ☐ No

Security

- ☐ Attendant - Hours _____
- ☐ Camp Host - Hours _____
- ☐ Gates
- Lock Out Times _____
- Opening _____ Closing _____

Connectivity   Signal Quality (circle one)

- ☐ WiFi   ☐ Free   ☐ Fee _____
- ☐ Cell Service Carrier _____
- ☐ TV   ☐ Free   ☐ Fee _____

Facilities

- ☐ Laundry   Cost _____
- ☐ Pool   ☐ Hot Tub
- ☐ Boating   ☐ Pet Friendly - ☐ Free ☐ Fee _____
- ☐ Gym   ☐ Free ☐ Fee _____
- ☐ Club House ☐ Free ☐ Fee _____

Food Options   Kids Activities

- ☐ Groceries   ☐ Restaurants
- ☐ Snack Bar   ☐ Other Shops
- ☐ Playground ☐ Parks

Local Highlights

Things to do/Recommendations

Rating (choose 1 to 5 🔥)

🔥 🔥 🔥 🔥 🔥

Notes

Campground Name _____

Address _____

Website _____ Email _____

Phone _____ Hours _____

Category

- ☐ National Park
- ☐ County Park
- ☐ Private
- ☐ Army Corp. of Eng.
- ☐ State Park
- ☐ BLM
- ☐ Province/Parish
- ☐ Other _____

Rates ($, £ , €) (circle one)

Daily _____ Monthly _____

Weekly _____ Long Stay _____

Services

- ☐ Electric Amp_____
- ☐ Water ☐ Dump Station
- ☐ Sewer ☐ Water Pressure ☺ ☹

Toilets

- ☐ Pit ☐ None
- ☐ Composting
- ☐ Flush

Showers

- ☐ Yes
- ☐ No

Security

- ☐ Attendant - Hours _____
- ☐ Camp Host - Hours _____
- ☐ Gates
- Lock Out Times _____
- Opening _____ Closing _____

Connectivity

- ☐ WiFi ☐ Free ☐ Fee _____
- ☐ Cell Service Carrier _____
- ☐ TV ☐ Free ☐ Fee _____

Signal Quality (circle one)

Facilities

- ☐ Laundry Cost _____
- ☐ Pool ☐ Hot Tub
- ☐ Boating ☐ Pet Friendly - ☐ Free ☐ Fee _____
- ☐ Gym ☐ Free ☐ Fee _____
- ☐ Club House ☐ Free ☐ Fee _____

Food Options

- ☐ Groceries ☐ Restaurants
- ☐ Snack Bar ☐ Other Shops

Kids Activities

- ☐ Playground ☐ Parks

Local Highlights

Things to do/Recommendations

Rating (choose 1 to 5 🔥)

🔥 🔥 🔥 🔥 🔥

Notes

Campground Name _____

Address _____

Website _____ Email _____

Phone _____ Hours _____

Category

☐ National Park   ☐ County Park   ☐ Private   ☐ Army Corp. of Eng.

☐ State Park   ☐ BLM   ☐ Province/Parish   ☐ Other _____

Rates ($, £ , €) (circle one)

Daily _____   Monthly _____

Weekly _____   Long Stay _____

Services   Toilets   Showers

☐ Electric   Amp_____   ☐ Pit   ☐ None   ☐ Yes

☐ Water   ☐ Dump Station   ☐ Composting   ☐ No

☐ Sewer   ☐ Water Pressure ☺ ☹   ☐ Flush

Security

☐ Attendant - Hours _____   ☐ Gates

☐ Camp Host - Hours _____   Lock Out Times _____

                                         Opening _____   Closing _____

Connectivity   Signal Quality (circle one)

☐ WiFi   ☐ Free   ☐ Fee _____

☐ Cell Service Carrier _____

☐ TV   ☐ Free   ☐ Fee _____

Facilities

☐ Laundry   Cost _____   ☐ Gym   ☐ Free   ☐ Fee _____

☐ Pool   ☐ Hot Tub   ☐ Club House ☐ Free   ☐ Fee _____

☐ Boating   ☐ Pet Friendly - ☐ Free ☐ Fee _____

Food Options   ## Kids Activities

☐ Groceries   ☐ Restaurants   ☐ Playground   ☐ Parks

☐ Snack Bar   ☐ Other Shops

Local Highlights

Things to do/Recommendations

Rating (choose 1 to 5 🔥)

Notes

Campground Name _____

Address _____

Website _____ Email _____

Phone _____ Hours _____

Category

☐ National Park   ☐ County Park   ☐ Private   ☐ Army Corp. of Eng.

☐ State Park   ☐ BLM   ☐ Province/Parish ☐ Other _____

Rates ($, £ , €) (circle one)

Daily _____   Monthly _____

Weekly _____   Long Stay _____

Services		Toilets		Showers
☐ Electric Amp_____		☐ Pit	☐ None	☐ Yes
☐ Water ☐ Dump Station		☐ Composting		☐ No
☐ Sewer ☐ Water Pressure ☺ ☹		☐ Flush		

Security

☐ Attendant - Hours _____   ☐ Gates

☐ Camp Host - Hours _____   Lock Out Times _____

                                      Opening _____   Closing _____

Connectivity   Signal Quality (circle one)

☐ WiFi   ☐ Free   ☐ Fee _____

☐ Cell Service Carrier _____

☐ TV   ☐ Free   ☐ Fee _____

Facilities

☐ Laundry   Cost _____   ☐ Gym   ☐ Free   ☐ Fee _____

☐ Pool   ☐ Hot Tub   ☐ Club House ☐ Free   ☐ Fee _____

☐ Boating   ☐ Pet Friendly - ☐ Free ☐ Fee _____

Food Options   ## Kids Activities

☐ Groceries ☐ Restaurants   ☐ Playground   ☐ Parks

☐ Snack Bar ☐ Other Shops

Local Highlights

Things to do/Recommendations

Rating (choose 1 to 5 🔥)

🔥 🔥 🔥 🔥 🔥

Notes

Campground Name _____

Address _____

Website _____   Email _____

Phone _____   Hours _____

Category

- ☐ National Park
- ☐ County Park
- ☐ Private
- ☐ Army Corp. of Eng.
- ☐ State Park
- ☐ BLM
- ☐ Province/Parish
- ☐ Other _____

Rates ($, £ , €) (circle one)

Daily _____   Monthly _____

Weekly _____   Long Stay _____

Services	Toilets	Showers
☐ Electric Amp _____	☐ Pit ☐ None	☐ Yes
☐ Water ☐ Dump Station	☐ Composting	☐ No
☐ Sewer ☐ Water Pressure ☺ ☹	☐ Flush	

Security

- ☐ Attendant - Hours _____
- ☐ Camp Host - Hours _____
- ☐ Gates
- Lock Out Times _____
- Opening _____   Closing _____

Connectivity

Signal Quality (circle one)

- ☐ WiFi   ☐ Free   ☐ Fee _____
- ☐ Cell Service   Carrier _____
- ☐ TV   ☐ Free   ☐ Fee _____

Facilities

- ☐ Laundry   Cost _____   ☐ Gym   ☐ Free   ☐ Fee _____
- ☐ Pool   ☐ Hot Tub   ☐ Club House   ☐ Free   ☐ Fee _____
- ☐ Boating   ☐ Pet Friendly -   ☐ Free   ☐ Fee _____

Food Options

- ☐ Groceries   ☐ Restaurants
- ☐ Snack Bar   ☐ Other Shops

Kids Activities

- ☐ Playground   ☐ Parks

Local Highlights

Things to do/Recommendations

Rating (choose 1 to 5 🔥)

🔥 🔥 🔥 🔥 🔥 🔥

Notes

Campground Name _____

Address _____

Website _____ Email _____

Phone _____ Hours _____

Category

☐ National Park   ☐ County Park   ☐ Private   ☐ Army Corp. of Eng.

☐ State Park   ☐ BLM   ☐ Province/Parish   ☐ Other _____

Rates ($, £ , €) (circle one)

Daily _____   Monthly _____

Weekly _____   Long Stay _____

Services   Toilets   Showers

☐ Electric   Amp_____   ☐ Pit   ☐ None   ☐ Yes

☐ Water   ☐ Dump Station   ☐ Composting   ☐ No

☐ Sewer   ☐ Water Pressure ☺ ☹ ☐ Flush

Security

☐ Attendant - Hours _____   ☐ Gates

☐ Camp Host - Hours _____   Lock Out Times _____

Opening _____   Closing _____

Connectivity   Signal Quality (circle one)

☐ WiFi   ☐ Free   ☐ Fee _____

☐ Cell Service   Carrier _____

☐ TV   ☐ Free   ☐ Fee _____

Facilities

☐ Laundry   Cost _____   ☐ Gym   ☐ Free   ☐ Fee _____

☐ Pool   ☐ Hot Tub   ☐ Club House ☐ Free   ☐ Fee _____

☐ Boating   ☐ Pet Friendly - ☐ Free   ☐ Fee _____

Food Options   Kids Activities

☐ Groceries   ☐ Restaurants   ☐ Playground   ☐ Parks

☐ Snack Bar   ☐ Other Shops

Local Highlights

Things to do/Recommendations

Rating (choose 1 to 5 🔥)

🔥 🔥 🔥 🔥 🔥

Notes

Campground Name _____

Address _____

Website _____ Email _____

Phone _____ Hours _____

Category

☐ National Park ☐ County Park ☐ Private ☐ Army Corp. of Eng.

☐ State Park ☐ BLM ☐ Province/Parish ☐ Other _____

Rates ($, £ , €) (circle one)

Daily _____ Monthly _____

Weekly _____ Long Stay _____

Services   Toilets   Showers

☐ Electric   Amp _____   ☐ Pit   ☐ None   ☐ Yes

☐ Water   ☐ Dump Station   ☐ Composting   ☐ No

☐ Sewer   ☐ Water Pressure ☺ ☹   ☐ Flush

Security

☐ Attendant - Hours _____   ☐ Gates

☐ Camp Host - Hours _____   Lock Out Times _____

Opening _____   Closing _____

Connectivity   Signal Quality (circle one)

☐ WiFi   ☐ Free   ☐ Fee _____

☐ Cell Service   Carrier _____

☐ TV   ☐ Free   ☐ Fee _____

Facilities

☐ Laundry   Cost _____   ☐ Gym   ☐ Free   ☐ Fee _____

☐ Pool   ☐ Hot Tub   ☐ Club House   ☐ Free   ☐ Fee _____

☐ Boating   ☐ Pet Friendly -   ☐ Free   ☐ Fee _____

Food Options   Kids Activities

☐ Groceries   ☐ Restaurants   ☐ Playground   ☐ Parks

☐ Snack Bar   ☐ Other Shops

Local Highlights

Things to do/Recommendations

Rating (choose 1 to 5 🔥)

🔥 🔥 🔥 🔥 🔥

Notes

Campground Name _____

Address _____

Website _____ Email _____

Phone _____ Hours _____

Category

☐ National Park   ☐ County Park   ☐ Private   ☐ Army Corp. of Eng.

☐ State Park   ☐ BLM   ☐ Province/Parish   ☐ Other _____

Rates ($, £ , €) (circle one)

Daily _____ Monthly _____

Weekly _____ Long Stay _____

Services		Toilets		Showers
☐ Electric	Amp_____	☐ Pit	☐ None	☐ Yes
☐ Water	☐ Dump Station	☐ Composting		☐ No
☐ Sewer	☐ Water Pressure ☺ ☹	☐ Flush		

Security

☐ Attendant - Hours _____   ☐ Gates

☐ Camp Host - Hours _____   Lock Out Times _____

Opening _____   Closing _____

Connectivity

Signal Quality (circle one)

☐ WiFi   ☐ Free   ☐ Fee _____

☐ Cell Service   Carrier _____

☐ TV   ☐ Free   ☐ Fee _____

Facilities

☐ Laundry   Cost _____   ☐ Gym   ☐ Free   ☐ Fee _____

☐ Pool   ☐ Hot Tub   ☐ Club House   ☐ Free   ☐ Fee _____

☐ Boating   ☐ Pet Friendly -   ☐ Free   ☐ Fee _____

Food Options

Kids Activities

☐ Groceries   ☐ Restaurants   ☐ Playground   ☐ Parks

☐ Snack Bar   ☐ Other Shops

Local Highlights

Things to do/Recommendations

Rating (choose 1 to 5 🔥)

🔥 🔥 🔥 🔥 🔥

Notes

Campground Name _____

Address _____

Website _____   Email _____

Phone _____   Hours _____

Category

- ☐ National Park   ☐ County Park   ☐ Private   ☐ Army Corp. of Eng.
- ☐ State Park   ☐ BLM   ☐ Province/Parish   ☐ Other _____

Rates ($, £ , €) (circle one)

Daily _____   Monthly _____

Weekly _____   Long Stay _____

Services   Toilets   Showers

- ☐ Electric   Amp_____   ☐ Pit   ☐ None   ☐ Yes
- ☐ Water   ☐ Dump Station   ☐ Composting   ☐ No
- ☐ Sewer   ☐ Water Pressure ☺ ☹ ☐ Flush

Security

- ☐ Attendant - Hours _____   ☐ Gates
- ☐ Camp Host - Hours _____   Lock Out Times _____
                                             Opening _____   Closing _____

Connectivity   Signal Quality (circle one)

- ☐ WiFi   ☐ Free   ☐ Fee _____
- ☐ Cell Service Carrier _____
- ☐ TV   ☐ Free   ☐ Fee _____

Facilities

- ☐ Laundry   Cost _____   ☐ Gym   ☐ Free   ☐ Fee _____
- ☐ Pool   ☐ Hot Tub   ☐ Club House   ☐ Free   ☐ Fee _____
- ☐ Boating   ☐ Pet Friendly -   ☐ Free   ☐ Fee _____

Food Options   Kids Activities

- ☐ Groceries   ☐ Restaurants   ☐ Playground   ☐ Parks
- ☐ Snack Bar   ☐ Other Shops

Local Highlights

Things to do/Recommendations

Rating (choose 1 to 5 🔥)

🔥 🔥 🔥 🔥 🔥

Notes

Campground Name _____

Address _____

Website _____ Email _____

Phone _____ Hours _____

Category

- ☐ National Park   ☐ County Park   ☐ Private   ☐ Army Corp. of Eng.
- ☐ State Park   ☐ BLM   ☐ Province/Parish ☐ Other _____

Rates ($, £ , €) (circle one)

Daily _____ Monthly _____

Weekly _____ Long Stay _____

Services   Toilets   Showers

- ☐ Electric   Amp _____   ☐ Pit   ☐ None   ☐ Yes
- ☐ Water   ☐ Dump Station   ☐ Composting   ☐ No
- ☐ Sewer   ☐ Water Pressure ☺ ☹   ☐ Flush

Security

- ☐ Attendant - Hours _____   ☐ Gates
- ☐ Camp Host - Hours _____   Lock Out Times _____
                                            Opening _____ Closing _____

Connectivity   Signal Quality (circle one)

- ☐ WiFi   ☐ Free   ☐ Fee _____
- ☐ Cell Service   Carrier _____
- ☐ TV   ☐ Free   ☐ Fee _____

Facilities

- ☐ Laundry   Cost _____   ☐ Gym   ☐ Free   ☐ Fee _____
- ☐ Pool   ☐ Hot Tub   ☐ Club House   ☐ Free   ☐ Fee _____
- ☐ Boating   ☐ Pet Friendly -   ☐ Free   ☐ Fee _____

Food Options   Kids Activities

- ☐ Groceries   ☐ Restaurants   ☐ Playground   ☐ Parks
- ☐ Snack Bar   ☐ Other Shops

Local Highlights

Things to do/Recommendations

Rating (choose 1 to 5 🔥)

🔥 🔥 🔥 🔥 🔥

Notes

Campground Name _____

Address _____

Website _____ Email _____

Phone _____ Hours _____

Category

- ☐ National Park
- ☐ County Park
- ☐ Private
- ☐ Army Corp. of Eng.
- ☐ State Park
- ☐ BLM
- ☐ Province/Parish
- ☐ Other _____

Rates ($, £ , €) (circle one)

Daily _____ Monthly _____

Weekly _____ Long Stay _____

Services	Toilets	Showers
☐ Electric Amp_____	☐ Pit ☐ None	☐ Yes
☐ Water ☐ Dump Station	☐ Composting	☐ No
☐ Sewer ☐ Water Pressure ☺ ☹	☐ Flush	

Security

- ☐ Attendant - Hours _____
- ☐ Camp Host - Hours _____
- ☐ Gates
- Lock Out Times _____
- Opening _____ Closing _____

Connectivity

- ☐ WiFi   ☐ Free   ☐ Fee _____
- ☐ Cell Service   Carrier _____
- ☐ TV   ☐ Free   ☐ Fee _____

Signal Quality (circle one)

Facilities

- ☐ Laundry   Cost _____   ☐ Gym   ☐ Free   ☐ Fee _____
- ☐ Pool   ☐ Hot Tub   ☐ Club House   ☐ Free   ☐ Fee _____
- ☐ Boating   ☐ Pet Friendly -   ☐ Free   ☐ Fee _____

Food Options

- ☐ Groceries   ☐ Restaurants
- ☐ Snack Bar   ☐ Other Shops

Kids Activities

- ☐ Playground   ☐ Parks

Local Highlights

Things to do/Recommendations

Rating (choose 1 to 5 🔥)

🔥 🔥 🔥 🔥 🔥

Notes

Campground Name _____

Address _____

Website _____ Email _____

Phone _____ Hours _____

Category

☐ National Park   ☐ County Park   ☐ Private   ☐ Army Corp. of Eng.

☐ State Park   ☐ BLM   ☐ Province/Parish   ☐ Other _____

Rates ($, £ , €) (circle one)

Daily _____ Monthly _____

Weekly _____ Long Stay _____

Services   Toilets   Showers

☐ Electric   Amp_____   ☐ Pit   ☐ None   ☐ Yes

☐ Water   ☐ Dump Station   ☐ Composting   ☐ No

☐ Sewer   ☐ Water Pressure ☺ ☹   ☐ Flush

Security

☐ Attendant - Hours _____   ☐ Gates

☐ Camp Host - Hours _____   Lock Out Times _____

Opening _____   Closing _____

Connectivity   Signal Quality (circle one)

☐ WiFi   ☐ Free   ☐ Fee _____

☐ Cell Service   Carrier _____

☐ TV   ☐ Free   ☐ Fee _____

Facilities

☐ Laundry   Cost _____   ☐ Gym   ☐ Free   ☐ Fee _____

☐ Pool   ☐ Hot Tub   ☐ Club House   ☐ Free   ☐ Fee _____

☐ Boating   ☐ Pet Friendly -   ☐ Free   ☐ Fee _____

Food Options   Kids Activities

☐ Groceries   ☐ Restaurants   ☐ Playground   ☐ Parks

☐ Snack Bar   ☐ Other Shops

Local Highlights

Things to do/Recommendations

Rating (choose 1 to 5 🔥)

🔥 🔥 🔥 🔥 🔥

Notes

Campground Name _____

Address _____

Website _____ Email _____

Phone _____ Hours _____

Category

☐ National Park   ☐ County Park   ☐ Private   ☐ Army Corp. of Eng.

☐ State Park   ☐ BLM   ☐ Province/Parish   ☐ Other _____

Rates ($, £ , €) (circle one)

Daily _____ Monthly _____

Weekly _____ Long Stay _____

Services   Toilets   Showers

☐ Electric   Amp_____   ☐ Pit   ☐ None   ☐ Yes

☐ Water   ☐ Dump Station   ☐ Composting   ☐ No

☐ Sewer   ☐ Water Pressure ☺ ☹   ☐ Flush

Security

☐ Attendant - Hours _____   ☐ Gates

☐ Camp Host - Hours _____   Lock Out Times _____

Opening _____   Closing _____

Connectivity   Signal Quality (circle one)

☐ WiFi   ☐ Free   ☐ Fee _____

☐ Cell Service   Carrier _____

☐ TV   ☐ Free   ☐ Fee _____

Facilities

☐ Laundry   Cost _____   ☐ Gym   ☐ Free   ☐ Fee _____

☐ Pool   ☐ Hot Tub   ☐ Club House   ☐ Free   ☐ Fee _____

☐ Boating   ☐ Pet Friendly - ☐ Free   ☐ Fee _____

Food Options   Kids Activities

☐ Groceries   ☐ Restaurants   ☐ Playground   ☐ Parks

☐ Snack Bar   ☐ Other Shops

Local Highlights

Things to do/Recommendations

Rating (choose 1 to 5 🔥)

🔥 🔥 🔥 🔥 🔥

Notes

Campground Name _____

Address _____

Website _____ Email _____

Phone _____ Hours _____

Category

☐ National Park   ☐ County Park   ☐ Private   ☐ Army Corp. of Eng.

☐ State Park   ☐ BLM   ☐ Province/Parish   ☐ Other _____

Rates ($, £ , €) (circle one)

Daily _____ Monthly _____

Weekly _____ Long Stay _____

Services   Toilets   Showers

☐ Electric   Amp_____   ☐ Pit   ☐ None   ☐ Yes

☐ Water   ☐ Dump Station   ☐ Composting   ☐ No

☐ Sewer   ☐ Water Pressure ☺ ☹   ☐ Flush

Security

☐ Attendant - Hours _____   ☐ Gates

☐ Camp Host - Hours _____   Lock Out Times _____

Opening_____   Closing_____

Connectivity   Signal Quality (circle one)

☐ WiFi   ☐ Free   ☐ Fee _____

☐ Cell Service   Carrier _____

☐ TV   ☐ Free   ☐ Fee _____

Facilities

☐ Laundry   Cost _____   ☐ Gym   ☐ Free   ☐ Fee _____

☐ Pool   ☐ Hot Tub   ☐ Club House   ☐ Free   ☐ Fee _____

☐ Boating   ☐ Pet Friendly -   ☐ Free   ☐ Fee _____

Food Options   Kids Activities

☐ Groceries   ☐ Restaurants   ☐ Playground   ☐ Parks

☐ Snack Bar   ☐ Other Shops

Local Highlights

Things to do/Recommendations

Rating (choose 1 to 5 🔥)

🔥 🔥 🔥 🔥 🔥

Notes

Campground Name _____

Address _____

Website _____ Email _____

Phone _____ Hours _____

Category

- ☐ National Park
- ☐ County Park
- ☐ Private
- ☐ Army Corp. of Eng.
- ☐ State Park
- ☐ BLM
- ☐ Province/Parish
- ☐ Other _____

Rates ($, £ , €) (circle one)

Daily _____ Monthly _____

Weekly _____ Long Stay _____

Services   Toilets   Showers

- ☐ Electric   Amp_____
- ☐ Water   ☐ Dump Station
- ☐ Sewer   ☐ Water Pressure ☺ ☹

- ☐ Pit   ☐ None   ☐ Yes
- ☐ Composting   ☐ No
- ☐ Flush

Security

- ☐ Attendant - Hours _____
- ☐ Camp Host - Hours _____
- ☐ Gates
- Lock Out Times _____
- Opening _____   Closing _____

Connectivity   Signal Quality (circle one)

- ☐ WiFi   ☐ Free   ☐ Fee _____
- ☐ Cell Service   Carrier _____
- ☐ TV   ☐ Free   ☐ Fee _____

Facilities

- ☐ Laundry   Cost _____
- ☐ Pool   ☐ Hot Tub
- ☐ Boating   ☐ Pet Friendly - ☐ Free ☐ Fee _____

- ☐ Gym   ☐ Free   ☐ Fee _____
- ☐ Club House ☐ Free   ☐ Fee _____

Food Options   Kids Activities

- ☐ Groceries   ☐ Restaurants
- ☐ Snack Bar   ☐ Other Shops

- ☐ Playground   ☐ Parks

Local Highlights

Things to do/Recommendations

Rating (choose 1 to 5 🔥)

🔥 🔥 🔥 🔥 🔥

Notes

Campground Name _____

Address _____

Website _____   Email _____

Phone _____   Hours _____

Category

☐ National Park   ☐ County Park   ☐ Private   ☐ Army Corp. of Eng.

☐ State Park   ☐ BLM   ☐ Province/Parish ☐ Other _____

Rates ($, £ , €) (circle one)

Daily _____   Monthly _____

Weekly _____   Long Stay _____

Services   Toilets   Showers

☐ Electric   Amp _____   ☐ Pit   ☐ None   ☐ Yes

☐ Water   ☐ Dump Station   ☐ Composting   ☐ No

☐ Sewer   ☐ Water Pressure ☺ ☹ ☐ Flush

Security   ☐ Attendant - Hours _____   ☐ Gates

☐ Camp Host - Hours _____   Lock Out Times _____

Opening _____   Closing _____

Connectivity   Signal Quality (circle one)

☐ WiFi   ☐ Free   ☐ Fee _____

☐ Cell Service Carrier _____

☐ TV   ☐ Free   ☐ Fee _____

Facilities

☐ Laundry   Cost _____   ☐ Gym   ☐ Free   ☐ Fee _____

☐ Pool   ☐ Hot Tub   ☐ Club House ☐ Free   ☐ Fee _____

☐ Boating   ☐ Pet Friendly - ☐ Free ☐ Fee _____

Food Options   Kids Activities

☐ Groceries   ☐ Restaurants   ☐ Playground   ☐ Parks

☐ Snack Bar   ☐ Other Shops

Local Highlights

Things to do/Recommendations

Rating (choose 1 to 5 🔥)

🔥 🔥 🔥 🔥 🔥

Notes

Campground Name _____

Address _____

Website _____ Email _____

Phone _____ Hours _____

Category

☐ National Park   ☐ County Park   ☐ Private   ☐ Army Corp. of Eng.

☐ State Park   ☐ BLM   ☐ Province/Parish   ☐ Other _____

Rates ($, £ , €) (circle one)

Daily _____   Monthly _____

Weekly _____   Long Stay _____

Services   Toilets   Showers

☐ Electric   Amp_____   ☐ Pit   ☐ None   ☐ Yes

☐ Water   ☐ Dump Station   ☐ Composting   ☐ No

☐ Sewer   ☐ Water Pressure ☺ ☹   ☐ Flush

Security

☐ Attendant - Hours _____   ☐ Gates

☐ Camp Host - Hours _____   Lock Out Times _____

Opening _____   Closing _____

Connectivity   Signal Quality (circle one)

☐ WiFi   ☐ Free   ☐ Fee _____

☐ Cell Service   Carrier _____

☐ TV   ☐ Free   ☐ Fee _____

Facilities

☐ Laundry   Cost _____   ☐ Gym   ☐ Free   ☐ Fee _____

☐ Pool   ☐ Hot Tub   ☐ Club House   ☐ Free   ☐ Fee _____

☐ Boating   ☐ Pet Friendly - ☐ Free   ☐ Fee _____

Food Options   Kids Activities

☐ Groceries   ☐ Restaurants   ☐ Playground   ☐ Parks

☐ Snack Bar   ☐ Other Shops

Local Highlights

Things to do/Recommendations

Rating (choose 1 to 5 🔥)

🔥 🔥 🔥 🔥 🔥

Notes

Campground Name _____

Address _____

Website _____ Email _____

Phone _____ Hours _____

Category

☐ National Park   ☐ County Park   ☐ Private   ☐ Army Corp. of Eng.

☐ State Park   ☐ BLM   ☐ Province/Parish   ☐ Other _____

Rates ($, £ , €) (circle one)

Daily _____   Monthly _____

Weekly _____   Long Stay _____

Services   Toilets   Showers

☐ Electric   Amp_____   ☐ Pit   ☐ None   ☐ Yes

☐ Water   ☐ Dump Station   ☐ Composting   ☐ No

☐ Sewer   ☐ Water Pressure ☺ ☹   ☐ Flush

Security

☐ Attendant - Hours _____   ☐ Gates

☐ Camp Host - Hours _____   Lock Out Times _____

                                       Opening _____   Closing _____

Connectivity   Signal Quality (circle one)

☐ WiFi   ☐ Free   ☐ Fee _____

☐ Cell Service   Carrier _____

☐ TV   ☐ Free   ☐ Fee _____

Facilities

☐ Laundry   Cost _____   ☐ Gym   ☐ Free   ☐ Fee _____

☐ Pool   ☐ Hot Tub   ☐ Club House   ☐ Free   ☐ Fee _____

☐ Boating   ☐ Pet Friendly - ☐ Free   ☐ Fee _____

Food Options   Kids Activities

☐ Groceries   ☐ Restaurants   ☐ Playground   ☐ Parks

☐ Snack Bar   ☐ Other Shops

Local Highlights

Things to do/Recommendations

Rating (choose 1 to 5 🔥)

🔥 🔥 🔥 🔥 🔥

Notes

Campground Name _____

Address _____

Website _____ Email _____

Phone _____ Hours _____

Category

- ☐ National Park
- ☐ County Park
- ☐ Private
- ☐ Army Corp. of Eng.
- ☐ State Park
- ☐ BLM
- ☐ Province/Parish
- ☐ Other _____

Rates ($, £ , €) (circle one)

Daily _____ Monthly _____

Weekly _____ Long Stay _____

Services

- ☐ Electric   Amp_____
- ☐ Water   ☐ Dump Station
- ☐ Sewer   ☐ Water Pressure ☺ ☹

Toilets

- ☐ Pit
- ☐ None
- ☐ Composting
- ☐ Flush

Showers

- ☐ Yes
- ☐ No

Security

- ☐ Attendant - Hours _____
- ☐ Camp Host - Hours _____
- ☐ Gates
- Lock Out Times _____
- Opening _____ Closing _____

Connectivity

- ☐ WiFi   ☐ Free   ☐ Fee _____
- ☐ Cell Service Carrier _____
- ☐ TV   ☐ Free   ☐ Fee _____

Signal Quality (circle one)

Facilities

- ☐ Laundry   Cost _____
- ☐ Pool   ☐ Hot Tub
- ☐ Boating   ☐ Pet Friendly - ☐ Free   ☐ Fee _____
- ☐ Gym   ☐ Free   ☐ Fee _____
- ☐ Club House ☐ Free   ☐ Fee _____

Food Options

- ☐ Groceries   ☐ Restaurants
- ☐ Snack Bar   ☐ Other Shops

Kids Activities

- ☐ Playground   ☐ Parks

Local Highlights

Things to do/Recommendations

Rating (choose 1 to 5 🔥)

🔥 🔥 🔥 🔥 🔥

Notes

Campground Name _____

Address _____

Website _____ Email _____

Phone _____ Hours _____

Category

☐ National Park   ☐ County Park   ☐ Private   ☐ Army Corp. of Eng.

☐ State Park   ☐ BLM   ☐ Province/Parish   ☐ Other _____

Rates ($, £ , €) (circle one)

Daily _____ Monthly _____

Weekly _____ Long Stay _____

Services   Toilets   Showers

☐ Electric   Amp_____   ☐ Pit   ☐ None   ☐ Yes

☐ Water   ☐ Dump Station   ☐ Composting   ☐ No

☐ Sewer   ☐ Water Pressure ☺ ☹ ☐ Flush

Security

☐ Attendant - Hours _____   ☐ Gates

☐ Camp Host - Hours _____   Lock Out Times _____

Opening _____   Closing _____

Connectivity   Signal Quality (circle one)

☐ WiFi   ☐ Free   ☐ Fee _____

☐ Cell Service   Carrier _____

☐ TV   ☐ Free   ☐ Fee _____

Facilities

☐ Laundry   Cost _____   ☐ Gym   ☐ Free   ☐ Fee _____

☐ Pool   ☐ Hot Tub   ☐ Club House ☐ Free   ☐ Fee _____

☐ Boating   ☐ Pet Friendly - ☐ Free   ☐ Fee _____

Food Options   ## Kids Activities

☐ Groceries   ☐ Restaurants   ☐ Playground   ☐ Parks

☐ Snack Bar   ☐ Other Shops

Local Highlights

Things to do/Recommendations

Rating (choose 1 to 5 🔥)

Notes

Campground Name _____

Address _____

Website _____ Email _____

Phone _____ Hours _____

Category

☐ National Park   ☐ County Park   ☐ Private   ☐ Army Corp. of Eng.

☐ State Park   ☐ BLM   ☐ Province/Parish ☐ Other _____

Rates ($, £ , €) (circle one)

Daily _____   Monthly _____

Weekly _____   Long Stay _____

Services   Toilets   Showers

☐ Electric   Amp_____   ☐ Pit   ☐ None   ☐ Yes

☐ Water   ☐ Dump Station   ☐ Composting   ☐ No

☐ Sewer   ☐ Water Pressure ☺ ☹   ☐ Flush

Security

☐ Attendant - Hours _____   ☐ Gates

☐ Camp Host - Hours _____   Lock Out Times _____

                                        Opening _____ Closing _____

Connectivity   Signal Quality (circle one)

☐ WiFi   ☐ Free   ☐ Fee _____

☐ Cell Service Carrier _____

☐ TV   ☐ Free   ☐ Fee _____

Facilities

☐ Laundry   Cost _____   ☐ Gym   ☐ Free   ☐ Fee _____

☐ Pool   ☐ Hot Tub   ☐ Club House ☐ Free   ☐ Fee _____

☐ Boating   ☐ Pet Friendly - ☐ Free ☐ Fee _____

Food Options   ## Kids Activities

☐ Groceries   ☐ Restaurants   ☐ Playground   ☐ Parks

☐ Snack Bar   ☐ Other Shops

Local Highlights

Things to do/Recommendations

Rating (choose 1 to 5 🔥)

🔥 🔥 🔥 🔥 🔥

Notes

Campground Name _____

Address _____

Website _____ Email _____

Phone _____ Hours _____

Category

☐ National Park ☐ County Park ☐ Private ☐ Army Corp. of Eng.

☐ State Park ☐ BLM ☐ Province/Parish ☐ Other _____

Rates ($, £ , €) (circle one)

Daily _____ Monthly _____

Weekly _____ Long Stay _____

Services   Toilets   Showers

☐ Electric   Amp_____   ☐ Pit   ☐ None   ☐ Yes

☐ Water   ☐ Dump Station   ☐ Composting   ☐ No

☐ Sewer   ☐ Water Pressure ☺ ☹   ☐ Flush

Security

☐ Attendant - Hours _____ ☐ Gates

☐ Camp Host - Hours _____ Lock Out Times _____

Opening _____ Closing _____

Connectivity   Signal Quality (circle one)

☐ WiFi   ☐ Free   ☐ Fee _____

☐ Cell Service   Carrier _____

☐ TV   ☐ Free   ☐ Fee _____

Facilities

☐ Laundry   Cost _____   ☐ Gym   ☐ Free   ☐ Fee _____

☐ Pool   ☐ Hot Tub   ☐ Club House   ☐ Free   ☐ Fee _____

☐ Boating   ☐ Pet Friendly -   ☐ Free   ☐ Fee _____

Food Options   Kids Activities

☐ Groceries   ☐ Restaurants   ☐ Playground   ☐ Parks

☐ Snack Bar   ☐ Other Shops

Local Highlights

Things to do/Recommendations

Rating (choose 1 to 5 🔥)

🔥 🔥 🔥 🔥 🔥 🔥

Notes

Printed in Poland
by Amazon Fulfillment
Poland Sp. z o.o., Wrocław